Lapping it Up

The Quick & Easy Guide to Making
Healthy Cat Food At Home

Patricia O'Grady

authorHOUSE®

AuthorHouse™
1663 Liberty Drive
Bloomington, IN 47403
www.authorhouse.com
Phone: 1-800-839-8640

First published by AuthorHouse   9/3/2009

ISBN: 978-1-4490-2434-5 (e)
ISBN: 978-1-4490-2430-7 (sc)
ISBN: 978-1-4490-2433-8 (hc)

Library of Congress Control Number: 2009909087

Printed in the United States of America
Bloomington, Indiana

This book is printed on acid-free paper.

While a properly formulated homemade pet food diet will reveal many external benefits
to your cat, and may even reduce the need to visit your vet, the Author of this book does
recommend that you keep in contact with your veterinarian for annual wellness check ups.

It is also recommended that before you make any change to your cat's diet or start any
new food regimen for your pet, that you contact your veterinarian first and discuss
the diet plan with him. We have seen great success stories from using this diet.

This book is dedicated with love,
to my brother Steve and his wife Evelyn.
They own the biggest cat I have ever seen!

Training your human is a thankless task.
"Why bother with it?" some kittens may ask.
The fate of the world is the issue at hand,
as felines worldwide stake a claim for their land.
From our point of view, we cats own the joint.
We lounge and sleep all day just to prove the point.

Some say the meek shall inherit the Earth,
but they've no fangs or claws, for what that's worth.
The cat is the ultimate species, you see,
we totally ignore man's authority.
These silly humans who can't play nice,
must understand we hate only mice.

We can leap and jump, even crawl up the tree,
Because we have nine lives you see.
Meow; call the fireman to help me get down,
Now I sit perched smiling, as I watch you all frown.
I'm the one that is really in control,
I'm just so good at playing my role.

Just what does training your human entail?
A host of fun things you must do without fail:
The sofas and rugs need a little makeover;
next it's time for a complete kitty takeover.
We sleep on clean towels placed in the guest bath,
and then make their best clothing a target of wrath.

Tear down those new drapes with a quick tug.
Then tatter the pile of the new Berber rug.
And when they are sleeping, you block off their nose,
paw at their lower lip, chew on their toes.

Strut on the mantle. If they give any flack,
knock down their trophies and all bric-a-brac.

Shed hair on mom's beautiful evening gown,
as she's headed out for a night on the town.
If they leave you home all alone for the night,
A human doing this can't be all that bright,
They're telling you by leaving, it's perfectly all right,
To totally redecorate 'til dawn's early light.
Knock things off the tables until they learn,
Hurry; go faster, before they return.

When they try to punish, you mustn't show concern.
All attempts of discipline a pussycat should spurn.
A snide flick of tail will convey no remorse,
but they will try harder to scold you, of course!
So, hide in the closet until they forget,
because everyone knows you are the favorite pet.

The felines have won,
but to the human's the battle's begun.
Pathetic and lumbering and clumsy to boot,
my friend, human dominance is really a hoot.
Cats take charge in your home! It's destiny, meow.
The verses above have already told how.
So sleep for an hour, and then grab some chow,
and start training your human, starting right now.

"Thousands of years ago, cats were worshipped as gods. Cats have never seemed to forget this."

Table of Contents

Introduction

After the great success of my book Woofing it Down, The Quick & Easy Guide to making healthy dog food at home, it has been requested of me to write this book for cats. I received so many wonderful messages from dog owners telling me how their pet's health improved, when they switched their dogs over to a homemade diet, and now I'm determined to do the same for cat owners.

All cats are members of the family Felidae. All cats share certain characteristics that are unique to the cat family. Cats are pure carnivores. They need a high level of protein in their diets, at least 30%, and lack the digestive system for a diet of grains, fruits or vegetables. Cats have powerful jaws, long sharp teeth, and claws that draw back into their paws when not in use, perfect for hunting their prey. Cats hear extremely well, and their eyes are adapted for vision in dim light for hunting just before dawn, and just after dusk, the prime hunting periods for them.

Interestingly enough, the cat family split from the other mammals at least 40,000,000 years ago, making them one of the oldest mammalian families. People have been captivated by the beauty and nature of cats for the last 4,000 years, ever since the first cats were domesticated in Egypt. They were introduced to Europe about 2,000 years ago, and came to North America when Europeans colonized this continent. In America, the domesticated cat is the most popular pet, and it is estimated in population to be around 60 million, according to the United States Census data. It is believed that almost 30% of all households own a cat. That's a lot of cats, especially considering that careful estimates place free ranging, feral cats to be around 40 million. Feral cats eat predominantly birds, rodents, and other small mammals. Domesticated cats, even when fed regularly by their human owners, still seem to retain their motivation to hunt. This has to make you wonder, if they are being properly fed, and are truly domesticated with all their nutrient requirements being met, why would they continue such a practice, especially when most aren't even hungry. I believe the obvious answer is the commercial cat foods we are feeding them, which have poor quality ingredients, and lack of understanding about what cats really need in their diet.

The life span of your cat should be at least 20 years. Your pet's diet strongly influences your pet's life expectancy, and it makes me wonder how long your cat would live if it was fed properly.

Do you know what's in your cat's food?

Go ahead and grab the bag, pouch or can of your feline's current food, and let's compare ingredients. Do you understand what those ingredients are? Some of the items commonly put into all the brands of commercial cat food will disgust you. Most of us like to think of ourselves as educated consumers. Sure we all read the labels on the sides of those bags, pouch's and cans. Don't we? Do we really understand what we are reading or have these company's tricked us with those television commercials showing beautiful prime cuts of beef, and fresh fish.

I'm sure that if people were truly informed about what their cats have actually been eating, most of these pet food companies would be out of the cat food business. I don't believe that anyone would willingly feed their cats something that was making them sick and in some cases, killing them. I'm going to tell you all the nasty little secrets of what's in these foods, and you're not going to like it.

The first thing you have to understand is that these companies are making the cheapest, most profitable cat food possible, with total disregard for the health and well being of your pet. They are in this business for one thing only, to make money, and that they are, pet food is big business. I know they want you to think that they really care about your cat, but the truth is ugly.

The truth is the cat food you are paying for with your hard earned money, the food your feline is eating right now, contains things like toxic chemicals, spoiled meat and waste and this is just the beginning. The sad part of this is, how these items get into your cats food in the first place and it will really surprise and shock you.

Commercial pet foods have only been around since the 1930's. They were born when cereal companies were trying to find something to do with their rejected grain, wheat's, rice, and corns that failed USDA inspection because of being moldy, rancid or had some other contaminant that wasn't safe for humans. They discovered that the meat industry was "wasting meats" that couldn't pass USDA inspection due to livestock that has been diseased. The fishing industry had some of the very same problems. They formed the moneymaking idea to mix these wastes and create a product called "pet food". They hired marketing firms to brainwash the public into believing that feeding their pets from the table, giving them human food was bad, and that their creation was the only nutritionally balanced food to give them. They created a processed artificial diet for profit, and made us believe it was the best for our pets. Sorry to tell you but we have been deceived.

Humans in the United States waste a lot of things and large corporations have figured out how get rid of all that waste, and make big bucks at doing it. We only eat the lean muscle from cows, fish, lambs and poultry. The remaining carcass is sent to a rendering plant, along with all other different kinds of waste, to be made into cat and dog food. This mixture contains, beaks, teeth, udders, lungs, intestines, heads, eye balls, blood, ligaments, tongues, chicken feet, hooves, spleens, unborn animal babies fetus's, hide, fur and more. The "meat" in those "meat by-products" in some cat foods may actually contain tumors, a "protein source" which is forbidden to human consumers, how disgusting.

If you don't like that, you really aren't going to like what I have to tell you next. The San Francisco Chronicle reported in 1990 that Dog and cat food could contain the remains of dead animals such as euthanized dogs, cats and horses. Although pet food company executives and the National Renderers Association vehemently denied the report, the American Veterinary Medical Association and the FDA confirmed the story to be true, and nothing has changed since. Yes, your cat right now may be an unwilling participate in cannibalism and unknowingly be eating another cat. These rendering plants sole business is to dispose of millions of pounds of dead cats and dogs and other animals that the government deemed aren't safe for humans to eat. Their end product is then sold to pet food companies. These rendering plants get their dead cats and dogs directly from dog and cat shelters. Most of these animals have been put to sleep and arrive at the rendering plant in plastic bags; many are even wearing leather collars, and flea collars. In one large city alone, two hundred tons of euthanized animals including dogs and cats are delivered to rendering plants just in one month. If over seven million dogs and cats are killed in dog pounds each year, how many of them have ended up in pet food. Amazingly, animals from research laboratories may be rendered into pet food as well, and still some insist road kill lands in some of the batches. So how do they label this on the bag? Why of course, it's called "meat and bone meal", and then they have another clever little term "meat by products". Another interesting fact is that meat and bone meal is thought to have been a contributing factor in mad cow disease. In

Europe they use meat and bone meal as a fossil-fuel replacement, and in America we are feeding it our pets. America needs to wake up and pay attention. Other countries aren't much better, and most are even worse.

Since the Mad Cow was discovered in Washington during December, 2003, the government has attempted to fix the shortcomings in the FDA testing processes, and to enact new regulations that will help protect the (human) consumer, but has done little or nothing to protect your pets. Mad Cow Disease is caused by rogue prions, the mutant proteins believed to be responsible for Feline Spongiform Encephalopathy, in which all forms of prion disease are fatal. The FDA has enacted new regulations for beef intended for human consumption, rendered meat by-products, including all those nasty things I have mentioned here, are still allowed in pet food, and those by-products could come from downer cows.

The FDA did conduct a study years ago looking for pentobarbital, which is sometimes used as a euthanasia drug, and they did find that some of the cat and dog foods tested positive for it. The ingredients that were most commonly associated with testing positive for the presence of pentobarbital were the meat and bone meal, and the added animal fat. If you give a cat a small amount of pentobarbital it will not kill him but is proven to cause seizure activity. The amazing part of this is, there are still no laws on the books to prevent these companies from doing this. Legally, pet food companies can dump just about anything they want into their next batch of cat food, and no one would be any the wiser. These laws need to change.

Let's discuss the actual meat that really goes into cat food. When cattle die, regardless from what infectious or contagious disease it suffered, their carcasses are salvaged by these pet food plants and used. These plants are not USDA inspected, but they claim that they are monitored from time to time and required by law to add charcoal to this meat, in order to keep these diseased meats out of the human food chain. In fact, this meat is labeled and stamped "unfit for human consumption". Which now by law makes it fit for cat consumption? Legally yes, with the charcoal added and all.

This meat is called 4-D meat; again let's cover this up and give it a different name, so that the public doesn't understand. What this name really means is that the cattle the meat came from were (1) Dead (2) Dying (3) Diseased (4) Down or Disabled at the time they arrived at the slaughterhouse.

Keep in mind, cattle which are sick or near death, are pumped with drugs like, procaine, penicillin, and several others in a last ditch attempt to save them, because it they arrive to the slaughter house as 4-D meat, they get less money for them, if any money at all. Therefore, all of these drugs as well as the possible infectious or contagious diseases that killed them in the first place are in the carcass after the slaughter.

These carcasses are more often than not contaminated with bacteria such as Salmonella, and Escherichia coli. Dangerous E. coli bacteria are estimated to contaminate more than 50% of meat and bone meal. These companies will argue that they cook this "meat" at 200 to 270 degrees for 20 to sometimes as long as 60 minutes, and that this cooking process kills all of these bacteria. This might be true to a certain extent, BUT it does not eliminate the endotoxins that some bacteria produce during their growth, and release when they die. These toxins can cause cats to get sick. Interestingly, the pet food companies are smart enough not to do any testing of their products for these endotoxins, most likely because they already know they will find them, and that would also be an added expense for them, which would cut down on their profits. As an additional note, when reading labels, the word "with" means that a pet food product is required to contain only 3% of the ingredient. The word "flavor" means that the pet food product is not required to have any of the ingredient in it.

The cat food companies want that cat food to have the longest shelf life they can give it; they want to make sure it can sit on a shelf in a store for around 1 year. To make the food edible (as if we could even consider it edible), fats used in pet's foods must be preserved with chemicals. Are these added chemicals safe for your cat? Not in my opinion. These companies add chemicals like BHA and BHT (which has been proven to cause liver and kidney problems. Some are adding Ethoxyquin, which is suspected of causing cancer in animals.. **Ethoxyquin is made by a chemical corporation to be used as a rubber preservative. The actual containers are labeled poison, and the department of agriculture calls it a pesticide. The OSHA lists it as a hazardous chemical. These are chemicals that are all banned in Europe. So you must be wondering how these companies are legally allowed to use this? They purchase items that have these chemicals already placed in them therefore they didn't add it themselves; these companies don't have to disclose that information on the package.** Propylene glycol another preservative has been known to cause destruction of red blood cells in dogs. I should note for you that propylene glycol was finally banned from cat food because it caused severe anemia in cats, but is still legally allowed in dog food, one small victory for felines.

Another added bonus in cat food is rendered animal fat. Rendered animal fat doesn't sound bad, but the real name for it is restaurant grease. Restaurant grease has become one of the major components of feed grade animal fat. This disgusting stuff is usually stored in fifty-gallon drums, exposed to extreme temperatures, sometimes outside for weeks at a time. This fat gets stabilized with powerful antioxidants so it doesn't spoil any further, and then is sold as a blended product to pet food companies. This is used to spray directly onto the cat food pellets to make bland, disgusting food palatable to felines. The fat also acts as a binding agent so that these manufacturers can add other flavor enhancers to trick your pet into eating it. Some manufacturers spray cat food with fish oils for the very same purpose.

Sweeteners are also added. Many cats like sweet tasting foods, just like we do, and pet food companies are going to add whatever they have that's cheap to get your feline to eat their food. Some of these companies have been known to add things like corn syrup, sucrose, ammoniated glycyrrhizin and some other sweeteners in order to increase the palatability to appeal to cats. They don't care that this additional dietary sugar has the ability to aggravate many health problems in cats, such as diabetes and obesity. These are commonly added to "kitty treats". This is certainly not good for your pet.

Sugar is another ingredient that you wouldn't think you'd find in cat food, but in a lot of the foods, it's there, especially in the semi-moist kinds. Some of the semi-moist foods can contain as much as 15% sugar. The sugar also helps to aid in bacterial contamination prevention. This amount of sugar can cause stress to a cat's pancreas and adrenal glands, thus causing diabetes. A cat should never ever have sugar.

Many commercial cat foods have added artificial coloring, and these have been associated with potential problems. FD & C red dye No. 40 is a possible carcinogen but is widely used to keep meat looking fresh. Blue No. 2 is thought to increase cat's sensitivity to viruses, but they go ahead and add that into the mixture. Another color that is commonly used and has not even been fully tested is Yellow No. 5. Several others were being using but finally were banned by the FDA. I'm sure that you must realize that this is being added for us, so that the food looks good, and we think we are giving nice pretty tasty healthy food to our feline. Believe me your cat doesn't care what color his food is.

Most dry foods contain a large amount of cereal grain to provide texture. These high carbohydrate plant products provide a cheap source of energy and they use it as filler because they don't want to use any more meat than they have to, so something else needs to be added to save them more money. Gluten meals are high protein extracts from which most of the carbohydrate has been removed. These are often used to boost protein percentages without the expense of animal source ingredients, like real meat. They have also been known to add hair to cat food, so that it will test higher for protein.

Soy is just another common ingredient found in my pet foods. It is used by the manufactures to boost the protein content testing, and also to add bulk. Tofu is good for humans to eat, but most forms of soybean don't agree with a cat's digestive system because it is unusable by the animal's body.

Corn gluten meal, and wheat gluten is also used to create the shapes of bites, chucks, and as a thickener for gravy in the canned or pouched food. I doubt that your cat cares about what cute shape his food is either, but the cat isn't the one in the store buying the pet food, you are.

Mycotoxins are also found in cat foods. What are mycotoxins? These are toxins from mold or fungi that are caused by some of today's modern farming, adverse weather conditions, improper drying and storage of crops which all contribute to mold growth. Pet food ingredients that usually are contaminated with mycotoxins are grains, wheat, corn and fishmeal, commonly used in cat food.

Pesticides and fertilizers also can leave residue on plant products. Grains that are condemned for human consumption by the USDA due to residue of chemicals or mold and mycotoxins can legally be used, without any limitations in pet food. Basically, not good enough for humans because it's dangerous, but we don't want to waste it, so let's give it to the cats and dogs.

So by now you should be wondering whom if anyone regulates the contents of pet food because this is insane. The AAFCO (Association of American Feed Control Officials, FDA/CVM (The Food and Drug Administration Center for Veterinary Medicine, and the PFI (The Pet Food Institute) are in the position of regulating the pet food business. There is NO requirement that pet food products have pre-market approval by the FDA. The present regulations pretty much say that almost "anything goes." The "meat" in those "meat by-products" in some cat foods may actually contain tumors, a "protein source" which is forbidden to human consumers.

So if these pet food companies are being regulated how do they get away with this? These agencies have set standards for cat food manufacturers to follow, but they DON'T have any authority to enforce them. This is only part of the problem. How many of these cat foods aren't even being manufactured in the United States. Most cat foods are being made in Canada and other countries something that no one really was aware of until recently. If these things are happening here, what do you think is ending up in the pet food from some of these other countries?

Pet Food Recalls

Pet Food recalls; what you don't know won't hurt you, or your pet? There have been several pet food recalls, and while some of them have been widely publicized, there are many that have not. Pet food recalls are far from new, many have been covered up and hidden, and if it happens on a busy news day, the story will never make it into the headlines. Bigger news stories take precedence, and after all it's only cat and dog food. As of the writing of this book, the most recent pet food recall of Menu Foods still leaves many questions left unanswered. No one wants to give a straight answer, and as the days go by the story falls from the news. Pet food companies are hoping that people will just forget about it, and most will.

These companies are going to work very hard on some more cute cat food commercials to pedal their products. The following is a sample of just a few of the pet food recalls that I was able to research, using information from the FDA, and I'm sure that I haven't found the information on all of them. No one has accurate numbers on how many cats or dogs have died from these recalled foods, but I believe the true numbers are so high it would make us all cry. When you take into consideration that most times when a pet expires, whether it's premature or later in life, we usually do not do an autopsy, even if the death seems unexplainable because of the financial expenses.

1995 Nature's Recipe recalled - Pets were vomiting and losing their appetite due to contaminated wheat.

1999 Farm Meats Canada & Euro can – Pig ears, pig skins, pork bone pet treats– Salmonella bacteria

1999 Doane Pet Care recalled - Contaminated with aflatoxin, corn based dry pet food. Products included Ol'Roy (Wal-Mart's own brand) and 53 other brands.

2000 - Iams dry food recalled - Excessive DL-Methionine Amino Acid, a urinary acidifier

2003 – The Pet Pantry International – recalled because it tested positive for bovine spongiform encephalopathy (also known as mad cow disease)

2003 - Petcurean Go Natural recalled - Was causing liver disease in some pets, but no cause was ever found

2005 - Diamond Foods recalled - Moldy corn containing fungal product aflatoxin

2005 – T.W. Enterprises treats recalled due to Salmonella contamination

2006 - Simmons Pet Food -Ol'Roy, American Fare, and

other pet foods recalled - Enamel lining in cans were flaking off into food

2006 - Merrick Pet Care recalled - Metal Tags found in some samples

2006 - Royal Canine recalled - prescription canned pet food - Vitamin D overdose causing calcium deficiency and kidney disease.

2007 – Nestle Purina Petcare, Hills Pet Nutrition, Del Monte Pet Products

2007 - Menu Foods recalled - over 95 brands including some of the top names in cat and dog food. Thousands of animals became sick and many died from renal failure. First they stated the problem was a pesticide, then rat poison aminoptern, was found in pet food at a lab in New York, and then it was wheat gluten. The last I have heard is that Melamine, which has a number of industrial uses, including use in manufacturing cooking utensils and plates, and fertilizers was found in the cat and dog food. Understand that if this food were tested, it would have made the protein level show higher; therefore, I believe it was added on purpose. The following is a quote from a CNN news source. "Somebody may have added melamine to the wheat gluten in order to increase what appears to be the protein level", the FDA'S Stephen Sundlof told CNN.

2008 - Mars Petcare US - Salmonella contamination

2009 – Nutro Natural Choice - This recall is due to incorrect levels of zinc and potassium.

No one wants to talk about it, and no doubt no one will be held to pay for the pain and suffering it has caused pets, and their owners. Will we ever get a true answer? Even with class action lawsuits being filed, no one will get rich over it because animals are considered property and you can't sue for emotional damages.

I don't know how a price could possibly be put on the death or illness of your cat or dog, because nothing can bring them back.

I find it interesting that the chief financial officer of Streetsville-based Menu Foods sold nearly half of his stock in that company just a few weeks before the company announced the recall in 2007. When he was interviewed about the sale of his stock he said, "It's a horrible coincidence, yes…. In terms of process, during any given year, we get consumer complaints all the time and it becomes matter of course for our technical people, so it's not something that necessarily gets flagged right to the top on an ongoing basis", Mr. Weins said.

So how can you be sure that your cat is eating something safe that is also good for them? The answer is very simple; you need to make your own cat food at home. You cook your own meals at home for yourself, doesn't your pet deserve to eat something that isn't going to make him or her sick. Making homemade cat food is not only very quick and easy; it's the healthiest food you can feed your feline. Many of these recipes can be made ahead of time, and frozen in meals, so that you only have to cook once or twice a month. Considering the food options choices on the market today for pets, I don't think people really have anything to think about.

Things you probably don't know about commercial cat food

Before the pet food companies were born, generations of cats lived to ripe old ages eating fresh foods. If your cat's food hasn't been recalled in the past, it does not necessarily mean that it is safe for your cat to eat. The majority of cat foods on the market today might not only be nutritionally void, in fact, they have no nutritional value at all, and could be dangerous for your cat. The best food to feed your cat is real food. While we think of this as people food, you need to think about it like this, we are not the only living creatures on the face of the earth that deserve to eat fresh food. It scares me to think that almost 90% of cats in the United States derive their nutritional needs from just one single source of processed pet food. Pet food is the most synthetic edible product manufactured, containing virtually no whole ingredients. Sure the packages tell you about all the vitamins they add, but the nutritional value provided by these foods will vary from batch to batch depending on the creation their animal protein made that day.

Naturally manufacturers claim that cats can thrive on a diet consisting of nothing but commercial pet food, but research and an increasing number of veterinarians implicate processed pet food as a source of disease or as an exacerbating agent for a number of degenerative diseases. Consumers need to be informed, don't be afraid to contact a holistic animal practitioner, or herbalist. I'm sure you are wondering why your own veterinarian hasn't told you about these dangers. You should take into consideration that veterinarian's knowledge of feline nutrition has usually been limited to the two weeks of nutrition that they had in veterinary school, and many of these nutritional classes are taught by direct representatives from pet food companies. Many vets office sell pet food, which seriously should be unethical considering the profit they make on it. Pet food companies will go as far as to hire students to be their representatives, and promote their pet foods to other students. This has become such a heated issue that it was placed on the agenda for an executive committee meeting at a major State University. The minutes from that meeting stated that a discussion was heard on how to handle dealing with pet food companies and their huge donations of pet food to the university. It was finally agreed to put together a task force to discuss the issue, however no further mention of this topic has been listed in any meetings since. I should note for you that after this meeting, a major pet food company, in an effort to "assist the university", and veterinary hospitals funded three new veterinary diet technician positions, donating over $100,000 to support these positions just for the first year.

I understand that it is hard to imagine that some of the big name pet food companies conduct cruel invasive tests on animals in their own labs, but it is happening, just for profit.

People for the Ethical Treatment of Animals (PETA) filed a claim with the FTC that dog food commercials were misleading. They based their claim from a ten-month undercover investigation of the research labs. PETA found this large pet food company was doing tests on dogs to find out how low quality the food could be, and still have the dog retain muscle mass. How they were doing this experiment was to cut chunks of muscle out of the dogs thighs, which PETA managed to capture on video.

Other things shown on the video were, dogs and cats circling in barren cages. Paws damaged from walking on the slats of cages. A lab tech overheard telling the undercover PETA worker to slap the dogs on the chest if they stop breathing. Dogs lay on a cement floor after their operations, unable to move. Animals with open wounds and hair loss, and animals clearly suffering from loneliness, and lack of socialization. PETA also further claimed to witness these other things, which weren't caught on tape, vets sticking tubes down animal's throats forcing them to drink vegetable oil. It was claimed that they overheard coworkers talking about a live kitten that had been washed down the drain. Workers having to leave work because ammonia fumes were so bad it had burned their eyes, but the animals stayed behind in their cages. Cats that only had a wood board to lie on, some having nails sticking out of them. Boards weren't even removed when one fell on a cat and crushed it.

PETA's investigator found at a different pet food manufacture lab, that many cats were lacking proper veterinary care. A kitten was even killed while having her blood drawn; the director of the laboratory believed that the kitten might have died because she was squeezed too tightly. Another cat had discharge coming from his eyes (a common problem—it was suspected that chlamydia was spreading around the laboratory), and the veterinary technicians missed several of his treatments, causing the cat to suffer even more. A cat used in their study, one that a PETA's investigator had befriended, had a large cut on his chin. The vet techs told our investigator that this unfortunate cat was "evil," and instead of treating the cat humanely, they put betadine in a spray bottle and tried to spray the cat in the face from outside the cage, squirting him in the mouth and causing him to salivate profusely. Later, the technicians indicated that the "problem was resolved," yet the investigator saw that the cut looked much worse and informed the lab's director of the cat's condition. Although the vet techs were told to euthanize the cat immediately, he suffered for five more days before the vet techs finally got around to destroying him. Do you really want to put money into theses company's pockets?

The best solution for your companion pet is to be fed only wholesome homemade diet, and I do understand that this involves cost and a time commitment, but if you do it, you'll see a huge difference in your cat's quality of life.

What a cat needs and doesn't need in it's diet

Cats are more selective about food by nature and anatomy. Their ancestral diet basically consisted of small rodents, and therefore their usefulness to humans had a lot of do with their willingness to get rid of unwanted rodent populations around human habitats.

You need to take environmental conditions into consideration as they can also affect a cat's eating habits. Some things that will deter a cat from eating properly are heavy-traffic areas in the home, loud noises, the presence of other animals, dirty food containers, or litter boxes that has been placed too closely to their food. You must be sensitive to your cat's eating behaviors and make any adjustment that is necessary to provide the best feeding conditions.

Cats are all unique and different and will vary in their own characteristics as far as the amount of food they need to consume to ensure their optimal weight and health maintenance. You must be very careful not to overfeed your cat, because this certainly will lead to obesity. Overweight cats are more prone to other health problems such as diabetes and arthritis.

If you have a finicky cat that refuses to eat, this can lead to other serious medical problems. Usually when a cat is ill, it will suffer from lack of appetite and therefore a veterinarian should always examine any cat that is refusing to eat and losing weight.

When changing to a homemade food diet, a difficult cat may refuse to eat, but can very safely handle the tough love 15 hour period of time without food that is often necessary to get them to accept their new food. The only time I would break this feeding stand off is in the case of a diabetic cat that shouldn't go without food for this long, and therefore it is understandably more difficult, but not impossible. If you have a finicky cat you may need to make the diet transition slowly, and have patience. Your cat may experience some mild diarrhea with the new diet change, but their stools will firm up within a few weeks.

Nutrition is one of the most important keys to your cat's health and longevity. You have the responsibility as a cat owner to provide your cat with the necessary nutrients required for its growth and maintenance. Before you can do that, you will need to understand exactly what a cat needs in their diet.

Meat

Cats are carnivores and designed by nature to be primarily meat-eaters. They are very different from dogs and people when it comes to their nutritional needs. A cat requires nearly five times more protein than a dog does, therefore it should equal a large part of their diet, and should be at least 60%. Cats rely on nutrients in animal tissue to meet their requirements. In the wild, a cat hunter would consume prey high in protein with moderate amounts of fat and minimal amounts of carbohydrates. I know that there are a group people who are praising feeding a complete raw diet, including raw meat to cats. They claim that this is good for the cat, since cats are natural carnivores. They will argue that out in the wild a cat would eat only raw meat, as they certainly couldn't cook it for themselves. I don't believe in this complete raw diet and I will explain why. The risk of infection by microorganisms and parasites in raw meat is high. This is especially true for cats that have a compromised immune system, autoimmune disease, a senior cat, and a cat that is on any type of medication. Cooking unlocks many nutrients in foods. But it also destroys some. My personal feeling is that there are more risks of bacterial and viral contamination in feeding a raw diet than there are health benefits. There is no reputable scientific evidence that cooked or raw is better for your pet, however there is evidence-proving risk by feeding raw.

You need to understand the meat that we go to the grocery store and buy is not the same meat that a wild animal eats from a natural kill. Commercial meat has been processed and has been exposed to many different factors, including chemical agents that make feeding it raw to our pets potentially harmful. Any vet will tell you that they have seen their share of cats and dogs on a raw meat diet come in to their offices sick. The risks you are taking feeding your cat raw meat aren't worth it. Do not feed fat by itself, as this can potentially lead to pancreatitis. Cat are known to get pancreatitis after they were fed the cooked skin of chickens and given too much meat fat. Choose better cuts of muscle meat, and trim as much as the fat as you can, and use little organ meats. Stores sell different grades of beefs, and keeping in mind that cats require more fat in their diet, you will want to use the less-lean ground beef, adding in additional chicken fat, beef tallow or suet.

I use the most commonly found meats, beef, chicken, lamb, and turkey.

Ground turkey should be purchased using 85/15 fat content, but make sure that you add diced dark leg meat for the added taurine.

Ground Chicken breast is usually 99% muscle meat with only 1% fat content. Ground chicken is usually around 15% fat, and you can use it the same as you would when preparing ground turkey. Make sure that you also add some of the dark meat from the leg, hearts, and gizzard, which will also add taurine.

Don't feed meats that can cause trichinosis like pork. In general, pork isn't good for cats, and I completely avoid it. I have found that they just don't seem to digest it properly. When feeding your cat poultry, try and feed dark meat rather than white meat. The dark meats have more nutrition and fat content than the white meats. Rabbit and venison also tend to be very popular with cats.

For anyone that is considering feeding his or her cat a complete vegetarian diet, I recommend that you reconsider your decision before your pet becomes ill. Cats were created as carnivores. They were designed to eat meat. One can argue if they are strict carnivores or just partially carnivores, but the answer is clear that they must have meat to survive. All you have to do is look at their teeth and that should remove any of your doubts as to what the Creator designed them to eat. I do not recommend an unnatural vegetarian diet for cats.

Fats

Even though you should be feeding your cat at least 60% meat or poultry in their diet, they will only be getting 10 to 15% fat content from that meat. This may be enough fat for a dog, but it is not enough for a cat, they require more than that. To add the proper amount of fat into your cat's diet you can add some fresh chicken fat or beef suet, and add a small amount of flax seed oil or coldwater fish oil to increase the omega 6 content. Do not use lard or any processed fats because they contain BHA, which is something that you want to avoid. If you are feeding too much fat you will know because it causes a greasy stool. As a general rule, your cats diet should be around 25% fat, and remember that chicken fat is much more nutritious for a cat than beef fat.

Carbohydrates

Cats lack many of the important enzymes that are necessary to process carbohydrates efficiently, yet most commercial cat foods are 35-50% carbohydrates, this commonly results in a cat developing diabetes. Cats are designed to utilize proteins and fats for their energy, not carbohydrates. The optimal diet for a cat is 5 percent to 10 percent carbohydrates; you must keep this to a minimum, no more. When they receive more carbohydrates than they need, the excess are stored as fat in their body.

You will be feeding only a small amount of carbohydrates, and they should be measured after added water and cooking. Rice is an excellent choice because few cats are intolerant of rice, rather than wheat, corn or soy. Rice also contains some of the others things that cats need like protein, phosphorus, iron, and some calcium. If you decide to use brown rice, it would be better because the unpolished rice preserves more of these important nutrients than the highly processed white rice.

You can try feeding a small amount of wheat in the form of pasta, using macaroni shells, but keep an eye on your pet for any allergic reactions.

Boiled potatoes can be fed in small amounts as another good ingredient for a cat. They are an excellent source of vitamin B-6, copper, potassium, manganese, and dietary fibers. Do not feed potatoes with the skin still on them, or those that are greenish in color or have started to sprout, remember that the goal is to feed human grade foods, not sub-standard.

Grains

Cats require almost no grains in their diet. A highly processed grain based diet fed to a cat that has a body designed to thrive on a meat based food diet will produce symptoms of ill health over time. I find it interesting that diets to address some of the diseases cats get always deal with the symptoms that are the direct result of a lifetime of the wrong food. Obviously the best diet for a cat should resemble one that is close to their natural diet. A diet that is balanced heavily toward grain promotes insulin production, and over production of insulin makes it very hard for the cat's body to maintain proper weight, and leads to diabetes. Also many cats have hyper allergenic sensitivities to corn, wheat, soy and yeasts, making them suffer from inflammatory Bowel Disease. A cat does have a small need for a certain amount of fiber however, but you must feed the correct kind and amount.

Fiber

Cats should have a little fiber from their carbohydrate source. On the plus side it will give them a bulkier stool, and can be helpful in pets that have constipation problems, are obese or in kidney failure. This should make up a very small amount of their diet, around 5%. Oatmeal fits this category well, and is a great ingredient for a cat that suffers from chronic constipation, so always keep this on hand. When your cat ingests fiber, it expends with water and helps to move and lubricate food down the intestine. Cats need only a small amount of fiber because their natural carnivorous diet contained less and their relatively short digestive tracts have less time to metabolize it. Some other excellent sources of additional fiber for a cat are rice bran, whole oats, canned pumpkin, beets, and carrots. Fiber seems to help cats with certain problems, including diabetes. Diets high in fiber seem to lessen blood glucose spikes. Another advantage of feeding a small amount of fiber is it will allow an overweight cat to feel full after consuming fewer calories, especially if you have a pet that clearly overeats. The best source of fiber to use in this situation is oat bran. Fiber can help with anal sac disease, chronic kidney disease, irritable bowel syndrome, and colitis. It is also very useful when treating Megacolon, a disease primarily seen in cats. Fiber can also help with hairballs, canned pumpkin for this purpose works great, just don't feed too much or your cat will end up with diarrhea, try just a teaspoon.

Water

Water is another element that is commonly overlooked. This is a nutrient that gives overall health; it helps regulate body temperature, digest food, eliminate wastes, lubricates tissues, and also allows salt and other electrolytes of pass through the body. Always make sure that your cat has fresh water available. Cats should never eat completely dry food. Urinary tract problems and kidney failure in cats have been closely related to lack of water. It's best for your cat to eat food that has water added into it.

Fish

Cats seem to love fish, but feeding too much of it can cause several problems, if it makes up too much of the cat's diet. Feeding your cat very small amounts of fish, as a treat once in a while is fine, provided it doesn't cause an allergic reaction. Many cats are sensitive or allergic to fish so keep in mind that fish is more likely to cause scabby, itchy skin and ears than other forms of meat. Two other problems with feeding fish are that cats seem to become addicted to fish because it is one of the more aromatic foods, and they love the taste of it. Some cats will often stage a hunger strike by refusing to eat anything else unless it has the flavor of fish; therefore I don't recommend feeding it more than once a week, and in very tiny amounts. It is also believed that feeding too much fish can cause urinary tract infections and blockages. Fish can be useful when trying to tempt an ill cat to eat, but a cat that eats fish all the time will also become immune to its appeal.

Another fact to consider is, toxic chemicals and heavy metal concentrations in fish are unpredictable, therefore is must be limited to no more than once a week, if at all. Avoid feeding canned tuna, cats that eat it, soon will want to eat nothing else, and don't thrive, due to high mercury levels and lack of other nutrients. Stick with fish that are caught in colder waters, such as halibut, salmon, pond raised catfish because they are higher in protein and omega-3 fatty acids. Salmon has the highest omega-3 level, and usually the lowest mercury levels.

Vegetables

Cats really do not need vegetables in their diet. You may witness a cat occasionally eat grass to clear their stomach of indigestible food, because it has a use from time to time. Eating vegetation in this way may aid the cat's digestive system and can prevent hairballs. A domestic cat has a larger intestine than is had in the wild, which allows it to eat more vegetation. Cats in the wild would also get a certain amount of vegetation just from eating the stomach contents of its prey. Many cats dislike any type of vegetation, and will only eat it if it's a matter of eating or starving to death. If you decide to feed your cat a very small amount of vegetables you must pick the correct kind, and that's only if your cat can tolerate veggies without getting diarrhea.

When feeding a small amount of vegetables, most cats have no problems digesting canned or cooked peas. They are an excellent source of dietary fiber. Cooked or diced carrots can be fed in moderation. Canned pumpkin can be added to your cat's diet for another great source of fiber, and many cats love the taste of it. Some pumpkin added into a meal helps prevent loose stools as well as constipation, so it can really balance them. Make sure that you use fresh pumpkin or pure canned pumpkin, not the pie filling which contains sugar. **Vegetables should not make up more than 5% of your cats basic diet.**

Fruits

Cats tend not to eat fruit, nor do they need to have it in their natural diet. There is no evidence that cats derive any benefits at all from eating fruit, therefore they shouldn't have it in their diet. Some fruits, such as citrus, grapes, and raisins can even make your cat ill. I have heard of some cats that enjoy an occasional snack of cantaloupe or a small piece of banana, but because your pet likes the taste of something, it doesn't make it good for them. I recommend feeding no fruit at all.

Eating plant matter, such as fruits and some vegetables alters the body chemistry of a cat and causes urine pH to be alkaline, which can cause urinary crystals. Urinary crystals in cats seems to be an epidemic disease caused by feeding the wrong diet, and it causes cats great pain and suffering, and can result in death. Feeding fruits can putrefy in the cat's digestive tract due to the cat's inability to break down this type of food source.

Eggs

Whole cooked eggs are an excellent source of complete protein and fat for cats. The protein in eggs is very high in quality, even higher than meat, poultry and fish. Cats can easily digest eggs, so they are a great protein source for them. Eggs should always be served cooked and never fed raw.

Eggs are an inexpensive source of quality protein, vitamin A, and minerals. If the eggs are free range they will also contain good amounts of fatty acids. Egg yolks are excellent food for your cat's skin. Today free-range eggs are becoming more popular due to demand. They are quick and simple to make and are also relatively cheap and quite healthy because the quality of free-range eggs is usually higher.

Free-range eggs are eggs from poultry, which have been farmed without intensive factory farming methods. The main difference between free range and factory-farmed eggs is that the birds are permitted to roam freely within the farmyard and only kept in sheds or henhouses at nighttime.

However, not all countries have legal standards in defining what free range means. The U.S. Department of Agriculture has no standards and allows egg producers to freely label any egg as a free-range egg. Many producers will label their eggs as cage-free in addition to free range, so that is what you really want to look for. Free-range eggs may have more of an orange color to their yolks due to the abundance of greens and insects in the diet of the birds. Do you have to use free-range eggs to feed your cat? No you don't, I'm just mentioning that I believe they are better.

I prefer that you serve your cat's hard-boiled eggs in their meal or scrambled eggs made in the microwave using no milk and no butter. Making scrambled eggs in the microwave are not only quick and easy, but they also cook up nice and fluffy. Eggs are the most under-rated foodstuffs there is, and you will see a big difference in your cat's coat when you add eggs to their diet.

Feeding your cat raw eggs is not something that I recommend. A lot of people, especially those that are following a complete raw diet for their cat feed raw eggs.

I don't believe in feeding raw eggs at all due to the risk of salmonella. Boiling the egg destroys and kills off any salmonella. Keep in mind that the risk of salmonella is even higher on the eggshell. So the safest thing is to cook the eggs before feeding it to your cat.

I recommend feeding your cat eggs at least three times a week. Calcium is one of the most important supplements to provide for your cat. I like to use finely ground eggshells because the shells are high in calcium and contain almost no phosphorus. By using finely ground eggshells as a calcium supplement you can more easily balance your cat's body so he has more calcium than phosphorus. You can also buy finely ground eggshells or you can make your own. Since you will be serving eggs twice a week, you can use those shells mixed into that same meal.

To make ground egg shells, wash the eggshells, and let them dry. Add the eggshells to a blender, grinder or food processor. Make sure that you keep grinding and grinding until there are no sharp pieces. The eggshells should become a powder. You can use a sifter or a strainer to remove any large or sharp pieces if necessary. If you don't feel you are able to get the eggshells fine enough, than purchase the ground eggshell powder. If you have a cat that is nursing or pregnant this additional calcium is something that their body really needs.

If you just fed the meat, carbohydrate and fat ingredients, your pet would not thrive. This is because red meat and fish are too low in calcium. Cats that lived on their own got around this problem naturally by consuming the bones of their prey in the wild. Meat and fish are also quite high in phosphorus, which inhibits the absorption of the calcium that is present in the total diet when the ratio of calcium to phosphorus is not the ideal, and therefore this calcium must be replaced. Most pet food manufacturers solve this problem by adding powdered bone meal or some kind of calcium carbonate to their food. If you believe your cat's diet is not high enough in calcium, you can add calcium supplements or just make sure you feed your cat eggs.

Milk and other Dairy Products

Adult cats that are fed the proper nutrition don't need milk, and many cats are actually lactose intolerant, which means that the lactose in milk products can often upset their stomach, it ferments in their intestines causing them diarrhea. Milk is not toxic to cats, and if you have one that has been getting it, and is begging, giving some of it a twice a week isn't going to hurt. I would suggest you use heavy cream or whole milk only, because the more fat that is in the milk means less lactose. Dairy products are an excellent source of balanced proteins and calcium, because they contain a protein called casine. You can also use lactose free milk products. Dry cottage cheese and farmer's cheese are also very low in lactose and can be added to a meal. You can also freeze low fat or no fat cottage cheese, and scoop off the separated liquid, which also eliminates all of the lactose from it. This will give you high protein content, which is exactly what your cat needs. Another thing you can do to add more protein, is un-pasteurized yogurt cultures, most cats handle this very well. These things are good to add to their meal, for additional proteins but must not be a cat's primary protein source. Cats that have been fed casine exclusively developed blindness and heart problems because of a deficiency in amino sulfuric acid, taurine. This is why you need to also feed meats, such as turkey legs, hearts, and gizzards, which are high sources of taurine.

Everyone asks how much should I feed my cat. It is very hard for me to give you a precise answer to this question without seeing your cat in person, and knowing its age. A cat needs approximately 30-35 calories per day, for each pound of body weight. If you have a cat that is extremely active, than obviously it will require more calories. If you have an overweight cat, than you will want to be careful about your portions, and naturally if your cat seems underweight, than by all means, offer more food. I do have basic feeding instructions in the recipes section. You know your cat better than anyone else, and you should be able to adjust your cat's food portions just from observing it while its eating, and keeping an eye on its weight.

Vitamins

Cats have special needs for vitamins, minerals, amino acids, taurine, fatty acids, niacin, and preformed vitamin A in their diet because they cannot convert beta-carotene to active vitamins, unlike humans that can, and cats also have difficulty digesting starch and other carbohydrates. All of these nutrients are essential for their metabolism, and they supply energy for growth and maintenance.

A veterinarian recommended multivitamin and mineral supplement along with digestive enzymes could also be added to your cats diet plan, but only if you feel your really cat needs it, as in the case of an extremely picky eater. There is no special need to add synthetic vitamins if you are feeding a well-balanced diet, because you are supplying your cat's nutrition with wholesome natural foods. You may want to consider adding additional antioxidants by feeding alfalfa, and barley grass.

When adding a daily vitamin, care should be taken because the problem with cats, is that although they need nutrients, vitamins and minerals, it is possible to give them too much of it, therefore it is important to know exactly how much they require. Too much vitamin A or D can be toxic, and I feel that your cat will receive adequate vitamin A from eating chicken, beef liver, giblets, whole eggs, and oily fish. Something else to consider is Vitamin D and A are stored in a cat's body so it does not have to be present in every single meal. You will notice that most of the recipes listed in this book have 100 mg taurine added to them. This is an important ingredient because meat loses much of its taurine content when it's cooked, therefore for a cats needs, this must be replaced. You can purchase these tablets either online, at a pet supply store or health food store.

Unlike dogs, what might be good for you and your dog could be detrimental to your cat, so you must follow the recipes in this book very closely, which will give your cat exactly what it needs.

Catnip

Catnip is a perennial herb that belongs to the mint family. The plant grows as a widespread weed in North America but was indigenous to areas in Europe before being imported into the United States and other countries.

The active ingredient in catnip, found in the leaves and stem is an essential oil called nepetalactone. It is believed that it was named for the town of Nepete in Italy, and Cataria is thought to have come from the Latin word for cat. The response to this chemical works through the olfactory system, that cats have a special receptor for. This chemical is actually thought to mimic the effects of a pheromone and causes a variety of different behaviors in cats.

When a cat encounters catnip, it will sniff it, rub it, roll over it, kick at it, lick it, shake their head and sometimes even eat it. Some cats will just go nuts over it, and than will finally seem to just lose their interest in it completely and walk away. It is actually believed that the sniffing is what causes a hallucinogenic high similar to LSD in a human, that lasts for approximately 5 to 10 minutes, however when eaten it acts as a sedative. This implies a general excitatory effect on areas of the brain, particularly those centered in and around the hypothalamus. Catnip is not an aphrodisiac; both males and females have the same reaction to it. Catnip has no reaction in humans, and some cats are also unaffected by it. Young kittens and older cats seem less likely to have a reaction to it. The effects of catnip do seem to change from cat to cat; as one may drool while another could become hyperactive or perhaps even aggressive. Catnip can also affect larger cats, such as the bobcat, tiger, lynx and lion.

Catnip can prove to be useful for a few common problems with a house cat. It's a great way to force your cat to exercise, because it encourages physical activity unless you allow your lazy cat to eat it, then you'll find him sleeping. Many adult cats will respond to Catnip in a manner that resembles how they acted as a kitten, jumping, playing and running around as if it was given an injection of kitty adrenaline. Also if you leave the catnip out, in a few hours, your cat may just return to it on his own, and play all over again.

If you have a cat that seems bent on the destruction of your furniture then Catnip may again be able to come to the rescue. Cats can be frustratingly picky about just about anything under the sun including where they want to sharpen their furniture destroying claws. It is not uncommon for a cat to damage or destroy a piece of furniture just because the owners finally gave up on trying to redirect their cat to the unused cat scratching post that set them back anywhere up to a hundred dollars and more. A good way to attempt to change this frustrating and expensive behavior is to rub some Catnip or Catnip oil on a scratching post that you are attempting to get the cat to use. Introduce your cat to the treated scratching post and see how he reacts. If all goes well, your cat will sniff and inspect the post and then begin clawing at it. After a few times (you may have to re-Catnip the post) hopefully kitty will be trained to use the post rather than the sofa.

If you've never used Catnip before and you have more than one cat it is advisable to try it out individually on each cat before introducing it to all of your cats at the same time. The reason is because Catnip affects some cats in a negative manner causing the cat in question to become aggressive rather than merely playful. Introducing it to your cats individually enables you to control the situation and keep a cat that may react aggressively isolated from your other cats. This of course means avoiding a possible catfight that could result in broken furniture, hurt kitties, which could even require a vet visit.

Growing your own Catnip plant can be rewarding as it can save you money, give you the satisfaction of doing something yourself and ensuring that you always get fresh, high-quality Catnip for your cat. A word of caution however; the exact kitty reaction you want to grow your own Catnip is something to be wary of. If you plan on growing your Catnip plant outdoors and other cats can access your Catnip garden then be prepared for unwelcome feline visitors. This may not be a problem for you personally, but cats are by nature territorial and if you have a cat that lives alone without the company of other cats this could prove to be an area of stress for your cat. Even if you keep your cat inside at all times, your cat may get agitated if it looks out the window to see another cat frolicking in territory your cat considers their own. If you choose to grow your Catnip indoors, be careful to keep it out of reach of kitty. Otherwise you'll likely have your cat jumping up on furniture even to the most out of the way place to get access to the tempting herb. Cats are great jumpers and not really known for respecting precious household knick-knacks. So if you do decide to grow catnip indoors for a cat that reacts to Catnip, be careful to grow it in a place that your cat won't have constant access it. A room that you always keep closed to the cat is probably the best solution for indoor grown Catnip. If you do find that your cat reacts positively to Catnip you should be sure to use it sparingly so as not to dull the effect which can be the result of overexposure. A good rule of thumb is to not treat your kitty more than once a week on average to Catnip. Catnip, it seems, kindles a little bit of everything, exciting cats and allowing them to let go of their inhibitions. Although some people may be philosophically opposed to the drunken, appetitive, and seemingly erotic state that catnip produces, it has not been shown to be harmful and may even be beneficial in some circumstances. Also, the analgesic properties of catnip may be helpful for cats in pain.

While humans can't use catnip for a euphoric state, it can be made in a medicinal tea to soothe toothaches, help coughs, and also has been used for a sleeping aid.

The Overweight or Diabetic Cat

Diabetes is without a doubt one of the most common feline endocrine diseases, and in many of the cases, it is directly linked to a high carbohydrate cat food diet. We humans seem to understand that diabetes is more common in people that are severely overweight, and the same is true for our cats. Just like our own bodies, adipose fat cells produce a substance that increases the resistance of the body's cells to insulin, which then causes Type 2 diabetes, the most common type of diabetes in cats. Cats that are diabetic or have any other medical condition should make the switch to a more protein based homemade diet under the direct supervision of a veterinarian. The worse thing you can do is continue to feed a cat with diabetes commercial cat food, the dry food being the very worse as its usually even higher in carbohydrates and other hypoallergenic ingredients, and species inappropriate things. You will find that most cats that are in a current diabetic state will no longer need any insulin when they are fed the correct low carbohydrate diet, or their insulin dose will be severely reduced. Make sure that you speak with your vet when you change your diabetic cat's diet over to this homemade diet, because he will need to reduce your cats insulin dosage immediately, with the ultimate goal being to completely stop it. This is very important otherwise your cat will suffer from low blood sugar, which can result in brain damage or death, due to overdoses of insulin. What you feed your cat has an immediate affect on his blood sugar levels, so you must make adjustments for this at the same time as you change the diet. Let me warn you here that many vets seem to greatly underestimate how much the insulin dosage needs to be lowered when starting a low carb diet, so please make sure you get a vet that fully understands the connection.

Carbohydrates themselves are not the only problem for a diabetic cat, but they play a significant part of the problem contributing to high blood sugar levels. If you lower the carbohydrates, you must lower the insulin to match it, otherwise you are risking the safety and health of your cat.

Every cat will respond differently depending on several factors, the net diets carbohydrate content, the carbohydrate content you were originally feeding, how quickly the cat responds to decreasing carbohydrates, how quickly you are able to make the change over to homemade food, how your cat reacts to insulin and it's current dosage, and so on. High protein, low carbohydrate, and low fiber diets are wonderful for the management of a cat's diabetes, and ideally you should keep all grains out of your cats diet. Feeding a homemade diet will be a little more difficult with a diabetic cat due to the fact that they must eat on a strict schedule, but it should be done, and the benefits will show quickly. When is comes to a humans diet, we know all about good carbs and bad carbs, but for a cat this isn't the case, because their bodies don't need carbs at all, therefore we only want them to eat the amount of carbohydrates they would naturally get in nature, not the created commercial diets we have been feeding them.

You can purchase an in-home blood glucose monitoring kit, so that you can monitor your cats insulin needs. I know that this sounds stressful and difficult, but it really is easier than you would think. I understand that in the past your cat's insulin dosage has been set and determined by blood tests taken over the period of several months at a time, but this isn't truly the safest way to manage a diabetic patient.

Due to the sedentary nature of house cats, it is certainly understandable why so many become obese. Just like humans, less physical activity, and eating more than they should, will make for weight gain. Not surprising, many studies have shown that overweight owners have overweight pets. If you have an overweight cat, you should consider switching your cat's diet to homemade meals, and be extra careful about portion size, before your cat has serious health problems.

Several studies have shown that cats that retain optimal weight during their life, live approximately two years longer, don't suffer from arthritis, have lower blood pressure, and maintain a healthy immune system.

If your cat just seems to overeat, you can feed it only two-thirds of what it is currently getting. You must remember that your pet isn't opening up the kitchen cabinets, and making it's own meals; therefore, you are part of the problem. Weight loss should be gradual, you never want your pet to loss it rapidly, your pet didn't gain it all overnight, and it shouldn't lose it that way either.

In the recipe section you will find recipes under special needs, one is designed for the purpose of weight loss; you will only want to use these for a short period of time. Once the weight loss has been achieved, switch your cat over to the regular diet recipes.

Foods Your Cat Should Never Eat

As you must certainly already be aware, some foods that are edible for dogs and humans can be dangerous for cats because they have a different metabolism. Some can cause mild digestive upsets, while others can cause severe illness or death. If you are going to feed a homemade diet, please make a copy of this and place it on your refrigerator for all the family members to see, and finally memorize it. The following list consists of foods that should never be fed to a cat.

Alcoholic drinks – toxic, can cause coma and death

Baby Food – Most contain onion powder which can be toxic to cats.

Bones from fish, poultry or meat – Can cause intestinal obstruction or laceration.

Canned Tuna – Can cause malnutrition – mercury levels are high

Chocolate – Toxic contains caffeine

Coffee – Toxic contains caffeine

Citrus Oil extracts – Causes vomiting

Dog Food – Shouldn't be feed constantly, leads to malnutrition

Fat Trimmings from meat – Causes pancreatitis

Garlic – Can be toxic in certain amounts, best to avoid

Grapes – Toxic, damages kidneys

Green tomatoes – severe stomach upset

Human Vitamin Supplements – toxic to cat's organs

Large amounts of Liver – Too much causes vitamin A toxicity

Macadamia Nuts – Toxic

Milk – Look for lactose free milk products for cats

Moldy or spoiled food – Only feed human grade fresh food

Mushrooms – Toxic, can cause shock and death

Onions – Damages red blood cells, causes anemia.

Persimmons – Causes enteritis

Pork – stomach upset

Potato – Affects digestive system

Raisins – Toxic, damages kidney

Raw eggs – Decreases absorption of vitamins, leads to skin problems

Raw Fish – Leads to thiamine deficiency

Rhubarb – Affects digestive system

Salt – Can cause electrolyte imbalances

Spinach – Can lead to crystals in urine best to avoid it.

Sugar – Leads to diabetes, obesity and dental problems

Tea – Toxic contains caffeine

Tomato leaves or stems – Affects digestive system

Beware of poisonous plants

Many plants are toxic to cats; some are irritants and others outright poisonous. Since cats can be curious especially young kittens, care needs to be taken with inside houseplants, and supervision for a cat that has free access outside. The following is a general list of plants that can either harm or be fatal if digested by your cat, and this isn't even taking into consideration that some of these plants have been treated with chemical pesticides and/or fertilizers.

Alfalfa, Almond (Pits), Aloe Vera, Amaryllis, Apple (seeds), Apple Leaf Croton, Apricot (Pits), Asparagus Fern, Autumn Crocus, Avocado (fruit and pit), Azalea, Baby's Breath, Baneberry, Bayonet, Beech, Belladonna, Bird of Paradise, Black-eyed Susan, Black Locust, Bleeding Heart, Bloodroot, Bluebonnet, Boxwood, Branching Ivy, Buckeyes, Burning Bush, Buttercup, Cactus, Candelabra, Caladium, Calla Lily, Castor Bean, Ceriman, Charming Dieffenbachia, Cherry (pits, seeds & wilting leaves), Cherry, most wild varieties, Cherry, ground, Cherry, Laurel, Chinaberry, Chinese Evergreen, Christmas Rose, Chrysanthemum, Clematis, Cornflower, Corn Plant, Cornstalk Plant, Croton, Corydalis, Crocus, Crown of Thorns, Cuban Laurel, Cycads, Cyclamen, Daffodil, Daphne, Deadly Nightshade, Death Camas, Devil's Ivy, Delphinium, Dieffenbachia, Dracaena Palm, Dragon Tree, Dumb Cane, Easter Lily, Eggplant Elaine, Elderberry, Elephant Ear, Emerald Feather, English Ivy, Eucalyptus, Euonymus, Evergreen, Ferns, Fiddle-leaf fig, Florida Beauty, Flax, Foxglove, Fruit Salad Plant, Geranium, German Ivy, Giant Dumb Cane, Glacier Ivy Golden Chain, Gold Dieffenbachia, Gold Dust Dracaena, Golden Glow, Gopher Purge, Hahn's Self-Branching Ivy, Heartland Philodendron, Hellebore, Hemlock, Henbane, Holly, Honeysuckle, Horse Chestnuts, Hurricane Plant, Hyacinth, Hydrangea, Indian Rubber Plant, Iris, Iris Ivy, Jack in the Pulpit, Janet Craig Dracaena, Japanese Show Lily, Java Beans, Jimson Weed, Jonquil, Jungle Trumpets, Lacy Tree Philodendron, Lantana, Larkspur, Laurel, Lily, Lily Spider, Lily of the Valley, Locoweed, Lupine, Madagascar Dragon Tree, Marble Queen, Marigold, Marijuana, Mescal Bean, Mexican Breadfruit, Miniature Croton, Mistletoe, Mock Orange, Morning Glory, Mother-in Law's Tongue, Morning Glory, Mountain Laurel, Mushrooms, Narcissus, Needlepoint Ivy, Nightshade, Oleander, Onion, Oriental Lily, Peace Lily, Peach (pits and wilting leaves), Pencil Cactus, Peony,

Periwinkle, Philodendron, Pimpernel, Poinciana, Poinsettia, Poison Hemlock, Poison Ivy, Poison Oak, Pokeweed, Poppy, Primrose, Red Emerald, Red Princess, Red-Margined Dracaena, Rhododendron, Rhubarb, Ribbon Plant, Rosemary Pea, Rubber Plant, Saddle Leaf Philodendron, Sago Palm, Scotch Broom, Skunk Cabbage, Snowdrops, Snow on the Mountain, Spotted Dumb Cane, Star of Bethlehem, Sweetheart Ivy, Sweet pea, Swiss Cheese plant, Tansy Mustard, Tiger Lily, Tobacco, Tomato Plant (green fruit, stem and leaves), Tree Philodendron, Tropic Snow Dieffenbachia, Tulip, Virginia Creeper, Water Hemlock, Weeping Fig, Wisteria, Yews (English, Japanese, Western and American).

MAKING THE SWITCH

You've read this far and are convinced that you want to change your cat from eating commercial cat food to a healthy homemade diet. I've already explained to you all of the dangers and risks of feeding your pet a commercial cat food and your ready to do this.

So many people are just sitting and watching their cats deteriorate on processed commercial cat foods simply because they don't know what else to do, and I don't think that they realize that there are other options. You now have the knowledge you need, and are taking your pets health into your own hands. In a short amount of time, you will see your cats health problems start to improve or completely disappear with this diet.

Making the change to your cat's diet is easy, but you do have to keep in mind that feline's need to have changes made in their diet slowly. Cat's digestive systems are quite sensitive and many cats do not manage well when they are first given new foods, if an instant change is done. Usually picky eaters will make the switch surprisingly easy, as they love the taste of these homemade recipes.

Constantly changing your cat's diet can be detrimental to their health and is unadvised by veterinarians. With that being said, you must be thinking than how am I supposed to do this is. In a simple word gradually! This is going to take a little time do it the right way. I can promise you that once you have made the compete change you will never look back. By gradually introducing these entire wonderful new home cooked foods to your cat, you will spare him the problems associated with indigestion, constipation, stomach cramps, gas, vomiting, and diarrhea.

The best way to make a change to their diet is to wean them off of the old food, as you introduce the new food.

Smaller sized cats will need you to make the change slower than a larger one, as they just seem to be a little more sensitive to changes in their diet. No one knows his or her pet better than you, and depending on the history of your feline, you may have to make more of a gradual change or move along a little faster.

In the beginning, try and keep the diet as simple as possible, choosing one of the easy recipes. Keep the first few meals small. You can give your cat 20% of the new food mixed with 80% of his regular commercial food.

In a few days when your cat has tolerated the new food, start increasing. At this point you should be giving your feline 40% homemade food mixed with 60% of his old commercial cat food. After a week or two, you can start adding other foods like eggs, pasta, and homemade treats. The object is to wean your cat off the commercial stuff and onto healthy food, so in 3 weeks you have your cat eating 100% homemade food, and 0% commercial pet food. Once you have made the complete change, throw the commercial cat food out so that you are never tempted to "use it up". I know it's hard to throw something out that you paid money for, and everyone hates to waste something, but the cat food is garbage and that's exactly where it belongs. A cat that has been on a homemade diet will have severe diarrhea if you attempt to put him back on commercial cat food because his body has become used to healthy fresh foods.

The next step is to start adding supplements into the diet, omega oil, eggshells, and vitamin supplement. You want to give your cat time to develop his digestive abilities for these foods, and also this is good time to watch for allergies in pets that have had problems in the past with food allergies.

This is a guideline for you to follow. If you see any signs of diarrhea then you are moving too quickly, slow it down. If you see that your cat is tolerating the new diet without any problems, no loose stools, than you can move it along as little quicker.

What you can also expect is a big change in your cats' energy level. You will see a noticeable change in your pet in just few days, even an older cat. The big change that you will notice almost instantly is that your cat's eyes will seem more alive and brighter. Your pet will not only be eating healthier but your cat will be happier, and he'll love you more.

Remember, you can do this!! Don't be intimidated; it's really not that hard, it's just something different.

Exercise for your cat

I think one of the most overlooked facts about cats is they need exercise just like dogs and people do. Cats have the reputation for being lazy house pets, just lying around or sleeping most of the day, but we as their owners have made them into that. Regular exercise can have wonderful benefits to your cat, regardless of their current weight condition. Cats can usually be tricked into exercise, if you make it into playtime, your cat will never know the difference, plus you will also be benefiting from the time you are spending interacting with your pet, and bonding at the same time.

A few creative ways to get your cat to exercise are toys. Purchase a toy that has the feathers on the end, and move it around like a bird, which will encourage your cat to leap and stretch. You can also use slither snake like toys, and use them to go down stairs, and allow your cat to chase them, they also work great over the top of sofas, and chairs, and will keep your cat interested.

You can set up boxes making a soft-sided tunnel obstacle course from them, cats love playing in these, and will entertain themselves for hours, while getting needed exercise.

Even tall scratching posts allows a cat to tone their muscles in the shoulders and back while stretching out for a good scratch on them.

I like to see a multi-tiered cat tree in the house, this will encourage your pet to jump from one perch to another during playtime, and this is an exercise that also improves balance and coordination, as well as toning muscles.

Remember that cats often enjoy chasing something; even a plastic cap from a milk jar can be used on the floor as a hockey puck. Another good item for chasing is a wind up toy car or mouse; anything that you think your cat will run after.

RECIPES

Pick several recipes that your cat really seems to like, they each contain entirely different protein and carbohydrate ingredients; therefore you will want to rotate them, this will give your cat access to a wide variety of nutrients. Many of these recipes will make enough food for several days, make sure you give the proper portions, and bag the remaining food and freeze in individual portions, so that you aren't cooking everyday. If your cat doesn't like chunky textured food, you can place any of these recipes into a blender or a food processor and puree.

Basic feeding guidelines for these recipes are as following: As a general rule of thumb you should be feeding approximately: small cat— 1/2 to 3/4 cup; medium cat—1 to 1 1/3 cup; large cat—1 1/2 to 2 1/4 cups. If you have an overweight cat you may want to feed a little less.

Jersey's Finicky Feast

Ingredients:
1 cup dark meat chicken
½ cup white rice
½ cup chopped cooked carrots
1 hard-boiled egg
½ cup low sodium chicken broth
100-mg. Taurine

Directions: Cook rice following package directions and set aside. Broil or boil chicken, and cut into tiny pieces, steam small sliced carrots, and boil egg in water. Combine all ingredients and serve.

Kitty Sole Dinner

Ingredients:
½ pound of fillet of sole
2/3 cup white rice
2 tablespoons parsley, finely chopped
1 tablespoon margarine
1 tablespoon flour
½ cup skim milk
¼ cur shredded cheddar cheese
1 tablespoon chopped liver
½ teaspoon iodized salt

1 hard boil egg, chopped
100-mg. Taurine
½ cup water

Directions: Preheat over to 450 degrees. Cook rice to package directions and set aside, along with one hard-boiled egg. Sprinkle parsley on sole, place in a greased baking dish and pour enough water into the pan to cover the bottom of the dish. Cook for approximately 10 to 12 minutes. Once cooked, break apart using a fork and set aside. In a small pan, melt margarine, and then stir in flour. Gradually add milk until the mixture thickens. Remove from heat, stir in cheese, cooked chopped liver, and salt until well blended. Combine fish, rice, taurine, and cheese sauce together and serve.

Easy Sardine Cat Dinner

Ingredients:
2 cans sardines packed in oil
2/3 cup cooked white rice
2 chicken livers
¼ cup chopped parsley
1 hard-boiled egg
100-mg. Taurine

Directions:
Cook rice following package directions. Boil chicken livers and egg. Place sardines, rice, chicken livers, parsley, taurine and egg into a food processor and blend.

Feline Cheese and Chicken Livers Dinner

Ingredients:
4 chicken livers
2/3 cup cottage cheese
1 hard-boiled egg
¼ cup biscuit mix
2 tablespoons canola oil
Pinch iodized salt
100-mg. Taurine

Directions: Boil chicken livers, Taurine and egg. Combine all ingredients in a food processor and serve.

Cat Beef and Oats Meow Dinner

Ingredients:
2 pounds grounded beef
4 cups rolled oats
2 tablespoons butter
2 eggs
1 cup carrots
¼ cup kelp powder
¼ cup bonemeal
100 mg. Taurine

Directions: Cook oats following package directions. In a large frying pan cook ground beef until browned. Scramble eggs using butter. Steam carrots in a small saucepan; add oats, ground beef, eggs, kelp powder, bonemeal and taurine, mixing well.

Feline Chicken, Rice and Lentils Dinner

Ingredients:
1 1/2 pound whole chicken
½ cup white rice
½ cup red lentils
2 cups water
100-mg. Taurine

Directions:

In a large pot boil whole chicken until meat is falling off the bone. Allow to cool, and strip carcass of meat. In a medium sized pot, cook rice and lentils. Combine chicken, rice, lentils, and taurine together and serve.

Tabby's Chicken Hash Dinner

Ingredients:
1 ½ pound chicken
1 cup brown rice
1 cup cottage cheese
1 hard-boiled egg
6 tablespoons alfalfa sprouts
100 mg. Taurine

Directions: Boil chicken in a large pot until meat falls off bone, cut chicken into small bites. Cook rice to package directions and set aside. In a food processor combine chicken, rice, cottage cheese, egg, alfalfa sprouts and taurine.

Pussycat Lamb with Clams

Ingredients:
½ pound ground lamb (yes you can substitute ground turkey or chicken)
½ ounce of chopped clams
1 hard-boiled egg
4 teaspoons olive oil
1/8 teaspoon potassium, chloride
1 teaspoon barley grass
1 teaspoon omega fish oil
100-mg. Taurine

Directions: In a large frying pan, brown ground lamb. Add the remaining ingredients and mix well. This can be put into a food processor if your cat prefers a creamer consistency.

Gourmet Creamy Feline Salmon Pasta

Ingredients:
1 pound salmon
1 cup cooked plain pasta
¼ cup cooked spinach
¼ cup shredded provolone cheese
¼ cup kelp powder
2 tablespoons alfalfa sprouts
100 mg Taurine

Broil Salmon, and prepare pasta and spinach according to package directions. Combine all ingredients together in a food processor and serve.

Meow Chicken Parmesan

Ingredients:
1 pound chicken
½ cup chickpeas
½ cup water
¼ cup grated Parmesan cheese
1 chicken bullion cube
1 teaspoon omega fish oil
1 teaspoon barley grass
100 mg Taurine

Directions: Boil whole chicken until the meat falls off the bone. Dissolve bullion cube in boiling water. Combine all ingredients in a food processor and serve.

Fiesta Kitty Taco Dinner

Ingredients:
1/2 lb. ground beef
1 tablespoon tomato paste
1 teaspoon corn oil
½ teaspoon mineral oil
1 corn tortilla diced into bite-sized pieces
1/2 teaspoon bone meal
1/2 teaspoon brewers' yeast
1/2 teaspoon iodized salt
1 teaspoon finely ground eggshells
2 tablespoons grated cheddar cheese
100-mg. Taurine

Directions: In a large frying pan cook ground beef until browned. Stir in tomato paste, corn oil, mineral oil, diced tortilla, bone meal, brewer's yeast, eggshells, and salt. Stir until well blended. Stir in Taurine, and top with grated cheese.

Feline Cornish Game Hen Dinner

Ingredients:
1 ½ pounds Cornish Game Hen
4 cups rolled oats
2 tablespoons butter
2 eggs
1/2 cup carrots
¼ cup kelp powder
¼ cup bonemeal
100 mg. Taurine

Directions: Cook oats following package directions. In a large frying pan cook ground beef until browned. Scramble eggs using butter. Steam carrots in a small saucepan; add oats, ground beef, eggs, kelp powder, bonemeal and taurine, mixing well.

Feline Holiday Rabbit Feast

Ingredients:
½ pound Rabbit
½ cup oatmeal
½ cup chopped cooked carrots
1 hard-boiled egg
1 teaspoon safflower oil
1 teaspoon finely ground eggshells
½ cup low sodium chicken broth
100-mg. Taurine

Directions: Cook oatmeal following package directions and set aside. Broil or boil rabbit, and cut into tiny pieces, steam small sliced carrots, and boil egg in water. Combine all ingredients together and serve.

Turkey Pasta Dinner

Ingredients:
1 pound ground turkey
1 cup pasta
1 hard-boiled egg
½ cup yogurt
1 teaspoon barley grass
½ teaspoon bonemeal
100-mg. Taurine

Directions: In a large frying pan cook the ground turkey until browned. Cook pasta according to directions, and boil egg. Blend all ingredients together in a bowl, and serve.

Yummy Pussycat Trout Dinner

Ingredients:
1 pound trout
½ cup oatmeal
1 egg
1 teaspoon sesame oil
100 mg. Taurine

Directions: Preheat oven to 350 degrees. Coat fish with beaten egg, and dip into oatmeal. Fry in a medium pan in the sesame oil. Cut into small pieces and sprinkle taurine on top.

Liver A La Kitty

Ingredients:
¼ beef liver
1 teaspoon canola oil
¼ cup kelp power
1/8 teaspoon Psyllium Husk Powder
1 egg
100 mg. Taurine

Directions: Preheat over to 350 degrees. Bake liver in a shallow pan with a few tablespoons of water so that it doesn't dry out. Drizzle top of liver with canola oil, kelp powder, and Psyllium Powder. Cook for approximately 20 minutes. In a separate pan, scramble one egg and set aside. Cut liver into bite-sized pieces and mix with scrambled egg and Taurine.

Finicky Chicken Stew

Ingredients:
1 ½ pounds chicken
2 grated carrots
2 ½ cups macaroni
2 tablespoons canola oil
1 teaspoon barley grass powder
100 mg. Taurine

Directions: Boil chicken until it falls from the bone. In a separate pot boil pasta. Combine chicken, pasta and remaining ingredients in a food processor.

Feast of Beef Leftovers

Ingredients:
1 cup cooked roast beef or steak
2 tablespoons oatmeal
½ cup beef broth
1 tablespoon dried barley grass powder
½ cup string beans
½ teaspoon ground powdered eggshells
1 teaspoon omega fish oil
100 mg. Taurine

Directions: Heat leftover beef in broth over medium to low heat. Add string beans, barley grass powder, eggshells, omega fish oil and Taurine. Remove from heat and stir in cooked oatmeal, mixing well.

Beefy Potatoes Au Feline Casserole

Ingredients:
1 pound ground beef
3 cups boiled sliced potatoes
½ cup creamed cottage cheese
1 teaspoon nutritional yeast
2 tablespoons grated carrots
¼ cup milk
¼ cup grated Parmesan cheese
1/8 teaspoon Psyllium Husk Seed Powder
½ teaspoon finely ground eggshells
100 mg. Taurine

Directions: In a large frying pan, cook ground beef until browned, and drain of grease, stir in yeast, Psyllium Husk Seed Powder, eggshells and Taurine. In a large casserole dish, layer ground beef, potatoes, cottage cheese and carrots. Pour milk on top, and sprinkle with cheese. Bake for approximately 15 minutes, and remove just as the cheese begins to melt.

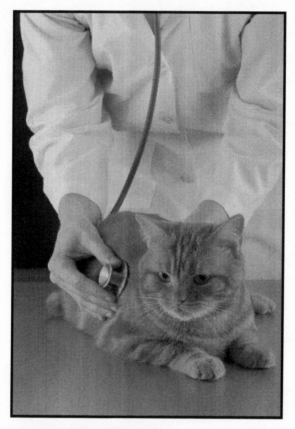

SPECIAL NEEDS RECIPES

Feline Weight Loss Recipe

This recipe should be used for a few weeks until optimal weight loss has been achieved, do not keep your cat on this diet for more than 4 weeks.

Ingredients:
¼ pound of ground beef, turkey or chicken
1 cup cottage cheese

(I recommend that you freeze the cottage cheese and than pour off the top liquid to remove the lactose)
3 cups of pureed canned pumpkin
1 can of peas
100-mg. Taurine

Directions: Slowly cook the meat in a skillet, until done. Remove from heat, and in a large mixing bowl, add all the ingredients together, stirring until well blended. Should your cat have any problems such as diarrhea on this recipe, lower the peas and pumpkin increase the meat and substitute a small amount of oatmeal.

Kidney & Bladder Special Needs Recipe

This recipe has been designed for a cat that is suffering from Urinary Tract Disease and/or Kidney and Bladder Stones, a common problem in cats. This diet works because it increases thirst, therefore your cat will drink more, and it doesn't allow stones to form by keeping the urine dilute.

Ingredients:
2 lbs ground beef
¼ lb of calf's liver
1 cup brown rice
1 teaspoon canola oil
1 teaspoon salt
1 teaspoon of phosphorus-free calcium carbonate (note that you can use 8 regular Tums tablets crushed)
100 mg taurine

Directions: Cook brown rice to directions on package and set aside. In a large frying pan, cook ground beef, and calf's liver until browned. Combine cooked meat with rice, canola oil, salt, phosphorus-free calcium carbonate, and taurine. Allow to cook and serve. Portion out the meals into Ziploc Baggies and store in freezer.

Low Sodium for Cats with Heart Problems or High Blood Pressure

Ingredients:
½ pound white meat chicken
2 cups of cooked white rice
2 teaspoons canola oil
1 teaspoon of flaxseed oil
1000mg of Calcium carbonate (You can use a crushed Tums)
100-mg. Taurine

Directions: Cook rice according to directions and set aside. In a large frying pan cook chicken in the canola and flaxseed oils. Combine with cooked rice, and add calcium, carbonate, and taurine.

Cat Chicken Diabetic Dinner

Ingredients:
1 cup chicken
1 cup chicken livers
½ cup oatmeal
¼ cup finely grated green beans
½ cup Unsalted vegetable broth
100-mg. Taurine

Directions: Boil chicken and chicken livers, and dice into small bite sized pieces. Cook oatmeal to package directions, and add grated green beans. Combine all ingredients and mix together with vegetable broth.

Diabetic Kitty Diet # 2

Ingredients:
½ pound ground turkey
1 large egg
4 ounces sardines
4 teaspoons canola oil
1/8 teaspoon potassium chloride
1 teaspoon bonemeal
100 mg. Taurine

Directions: In a large frying pan, cook turkey until browned. Boil on egg until cooked, and peel. Combine all ingredients in a food processor and serve.

My Cat is Allergic to Everything Diet

Ingredients:
2 pounds of lamb
2 cups brown rice
2 tablespoons safflower oil
100-mg. Taurine

Directions: Cook rice following the package directions. Broil lamb, let cool and place into food processor, along with rice, adding safflower oil and taurine.

Restricted Protein Feline Diet

Ingredients:
1/4 lb. cooked liver
1 large egg, hard-cooked
2 cups cooked rice

1 tablespoon vegetable oil

2 tablespoons water

1 teaspoon calcium carbonate

100 mg. Taurine

Directions: In a frying pan, heat the vegetable oil, and cook liver. Cook rice according to package directions. In a food processor combine all ingredients and serve.

Diabetic Kitty Treat

*Note this is for a snack treat, not a meal.

Ingredients:

3 cups oatmeal

1 ½ cups whole-wheat flour

1 cup water

1 tablespoon parsley

2 egg yolks

1 teaspoon baking soda

Directions: Preheat oven to 350 degrees. In a mixing bowl, combine all ingredients. Spoon onto a greased cookie sheet and bake for 10-12 minutes.

Cat Treats

It's fine to indulge your cat in a treat from time to time, but you need to keep a few things in mind when doing so. Treats should be just that, a treat and fed only occasionally. They should never be used as a steady diet for your cat, because they usually lack many of the proper basic nutrients a cat requires to maintain its health. Treats should never exceed more than 5% of a cat's daily diet. Keeping that in mind, most of the commercial cat treats on the market contain many of the same things that cat food has, and I can't recommend them to you. I have included several recipes in this book to make homemade cat treats that are much healthier for your pet.

Remember that none of these recipes have any unnatural preservatives in them; they will turn moldy if you don't store them properly. They should all be stored in airtight containers in the refrigerator, and can be frozen and defrosted as needed.

Cheese Ball Treats

Ingredients:
¾ cup white flour
¾ cup cheddar cheese shredded
5 tablespoons Parmesan cheese
¼ cup unflavored yogurt
¼ cup cornmeal
Tsp. water

Directions:
Preheat oven to 350 degrees. In a small mixing bowl combine cheeses, water, and yogurt, until well blended. Slowly add flour and cornmeal. Hand knead dough, and roll into small balls, dropping on a greased cookie sheet. Bake for 20 minutes.

Catnip Kitty Cookies

Ingredients:
1 cup whole-wheat flour
¼ cup soy flour
1 teaspoon catnip
1 egg
1/3 cup milk
2 tablespoons wheat germ
1/3 cup powdered milk

1 tablespoon molasses

2 tablespoons butter

Directions:

Preheat oven to 350 degrees. In a medium-mixing bowl, combine dry ingredients, flours, catnip, powdered milk, wheat germ, and set aside. In large mixing bowl, combine egg, milk, molasses and butter. Slowly add dry ingredients to wet until well blended. Roll dough on a lightly floured board with a rolling pin. Use small cookie cutters to make shapes and drop onto a greased cookie sheet for baking. Bake for 14 minutes.

Crunchy Oatmeal Tuna Treats

Ingredients:

1 can of tuna (packed in oil)

½ cup whole-wheat flour

½ cup nonfat powdered milk

¼ cup rolled oats oatmeal (uncooked)

¼ cup cornmeal

1 tablespoon vegetable oil

½ tablespoon brewers yeast

1 medium egg

½ cup unsalted chicken broth

Directions: Preheat over to 350 degrees. Drain tuna. In a small mixing bowl, break up tuna with a fork, and set aside. In a medium-mixing bowl, mix together flour, powdered milk, oatmeal, cornmeal, and brewers yeast. Slowly add egg, oil, chicken broth, and tuna, blending well until it becomes a sticky dough. Place dough on a lightly floured board, and kneed until you have a smooth texture. Use a teaspoon to roll dough into small balls and place on a greased cookie sheet. Bake for 12 minutes.

Baby Food Treats

Ingredients:
1 Jar of Baby food Meat (beef, chicken, ham, lamp, turkey or veal)
1 egg
½ cup wheat germ
½ cup non-fat milk powder

Directions:
Preheat oven to 350 degrees. In a small mixing bowl, blend the ingredients together using a spatula. Roll into small balls and drop on a greased cookie sheet. Bake for 12 minutes.

Kitty Mackerel Heaven

Ingredients:
1/2 cup canned mackerel (packed in oil)
1 cup whole-grain breadcrumbs
1 tablespoon vegetable oil
1 large egg
1/2 teaspoon Brewer's yeast

Directions:
Preheat oven to 350 degrees. Drain mackerel and place into a mixing bowl, breaking it up well, using a fork. Add breadcrumbs, vegetable oil, egg and brewer's yeast, combining together until well blended. Drop ½ teaspoons of batter onto a greased cookie sheet. Bake for approximately 8 minutes.

Tasty Tuna Ball Treats

Ingredients:
½ cup whole-wheat flour
½ cup non-fat powdered milk
½ can tuna fish packed in oil
1 tablespoon canola or flaxseed oil
¼ cup of water
1 egg

Directions:
Preheat oven to 350 degrees. In a mixing bowl, break up the tuna with a fork, mashing it as best you can. Add the flour, powdered milk and mix well. Add water, oil, and egg, using a hand whisk. Roll into balls, and drop of a greased cookie sheet. Bake for 10 minutes.

Easy Feline Salmon Treats

Ingredients:
One 12oz. Can salmon
½ cup of flour
½ cup of oatmeal
1 egg

Directions: Preheat oven to 350 degrees. In a food processor combine egg and salmon until creamy. Slowly add flour and oatmeal until well blended. On a greased cookie sheet, drop small balls of batter and bake for 15 minutes.

Salmon Kitty Balls

Ingredients:

2 small cans Salmon
2 cups oatmeal
1 cup whole wheat flour
1 cup cornmeal
1 Egg
2 tablespoons sesame oil
1 cup unsalted chicken broth

Directions: Preheat oven to 325 degrees. In a large mixing bowl, combine all ingredients until well blended. Roll into balls and bake on a non-stick cookie sheet for 12 minutes.

Kitty Honey of a Treat

Ingredients:
2 cups whole-wheat flour
½ cup soybean flour
1 cup milk
1 tablespoon honey
1 tablespoon canola oil

Directions: Preheat oven to 400 degrees. In a medium-mixing bowl, combine flours. Slowly add milk, and honey, mixing well. Cover bowl with towel for 20 minutes. Add canola oil, recover with towel, and allow dough to rest for 40 minutes. Using a teaspoon, drop small balls of dough onto a cookie sheet and bake for 14 minutes.

Catnip Molasses Cookies

Ingredients:
1 cup regular all purpose flour
¼ cup of whole-wheat flour

2 tablespoons wheat germ

3 tablespoons catnip

1/3 cup of milk

2 tablespoon vegetable oil

1 tablespoon molasses

1 egg

Directions:

Preheat over to 350 degrees. In a medium size mixing bowl combine, flour, wheat germ and catnip, set aside. In a medium size-mixing bowl combine egg, milk, vegetable oil, and molasses. Slowly add the dry ingredients to the wet ingredients until well blended. Place dough on a lightly floured board; use a rolling pin to form the dough into a sheet approximately ¼ of an inch thick. Use small cookie cutters to cut shapes, and place on a lightly greased cookie sheet for baking. Bake cookies for 12 minutes.

Chicken Liver Delight Feline Cookies

Ingredients:

2 cups flour

1 cup cornmeal

1 egg

3 tablespoons canola oil

½ cup unsalted chicken broth

2 teaspoons dried parsley

1 cup diced cooked chicken livers

1 teaspoon brown sugar

1 cup mashed cooked mixed vegetables

Cookie Cutters

Directions:

Preheat over to 400 degrees. In a mixing bowl combine flour and cornmeal. In a separate mixing bowl, beat egg with oil, slowly adding broth and parsley. Slowly add the dry mixture, finally adding the chicken livers. On a floured board, knead dough into a large ball. Using a rolling pin, roll dough out to a ½ inch thickness, and cut into shapes, placing on a greased cookie sheet. Bake for 12 minutes.

Teenie Weenie Kitty Zucchini Oatmeal Treats

Ingredients:
Non-stick cooking spray
½ cup vegetable oil
¾ cup honey
1 egg
1 cup whole-wheat flour
1 cup white flour
1 teaspoon baking soda
1 teaspoon cinnamon
1 cup grated zucchini
1 cup quick oats oatmeal

Directions: Preheat the oven to 375 degrees. In a large mixing bowl, beat together vegetable oil, honey and egg, baking soda, cinnamon and zucchini. Fold in the oatmeal. Drop by teaspoon onto a sprayed cookie sheet. Bake for 8 to 10 minutes.

Cats Pumpkin Oatmeal Bites

Ingredients:
Non-stick cooking spray
¾ pumpkin puree
1 egg

¼ cup canola oil

¼ cup honey

2 cups quick oats oatmeal

½ cup sunflower seeds or flaxseeds

1 teaspoon cinnamon

Directions: Preheat oven to 350 degrees. In a large mixing bowl, blend pumpkin, egg, oil, and honey using a hand mixer. Add the oatmeal, seeds, and cinnamon mixing well. Spread the mixture into a 15 ½ X 10 ½ pan that has been sprayed with the non-stick cooking spray. Bake for 40 minutes or until golden brown. Let cool, and cut into bite size pieces.

Yummy Liver Brownies

Ingredients:

Non-stick cooking spray

3 tablespoons wheat germ

1 pound of liver

1½ cups flour

1 cup cornmeal

1 teaspoon water

Directions: Preheat oven at 350 degrees. In your food processor, puree liver. Add flour and cornmeal, and water mixing well. Spray a cookie sheet with non-stick cooking oil, and spread out, make sure that you press this down. Sprinkle the top with wheat germ. Bake for 20 minutes. Let it cool, cut into bite size chucks. This needs to be refrigerated and it freezes well.

Precious Kitty Pumpkin Treats

Ingredients:

Non-stick cooking spray

One 15 oz can of mashed pumpkin (do not use spiced pie filling)

1 teaspoon of vanilla

¾ cup Cream of Rice cereal (use can use baby cereal)

½ cup powdered dry milk

Directions: Preheat oven to 300 degrees. In a large mixing bowl, mix all ingredients using a hand mixer. Drop treats using a teaspoon on a cookie sheet that has been sprayed with non-stick cooking spray. Bake for 15-18 minutes. If you want a bigger size treat, drop using a tablespoon.

Parmesan Cheese Biscuits

Ingredients:

2 cups whole-wheat flour

1 /3 cup vegetable oil

1/3 cup powdered milk

1 egg

½ cup of grated Parmesan cheese

Directions: Preheat oven to 350 degrees. In a large mixing bowl, combine all ingredients using a hand mixer. This will make nice stiff dough. Roll out dough on a floured board, and cut out shapes using cookie cutters. Bake on cookie sheets for 16 to 18 minutes.

Happy Birthday Kitty Carrot Cake

It's your cat's birthday let him eat cake!! The human guests at his party will also enjoy a slice.

Ingredients:
2 large eggs
½ cup plain nonfat yogurt
3 tablespoons canola oil
½ cup unsweetened applesauce
2 teaspoons vanilla extract
2-½ cups unbleached flour or whole-wheat flour
2 teaspoons baking powder

1/3-cup honey
½ teaspoon baking soda
1 teaspoon ground cinnamon
1 cup shredded carrots
4 ounces unsweetened crushed pineapple with juice
Cream Cheese

Directions:

Preheat oven to 400 degrees. Position the top rack in the center of the oven. In a mixing bowl, whisk together the eggs, yogurt, oil, applesauce, honey, and vanilla. In a separate bowl sift together, flour, baking powder, baking soda, cinnamon. With a hand mixer, gradually add the dry ingredients into the wet mixture. By hand, stir in the shredded carrots. Drain the juice from the pineapple, and stir into the mixture. Lightly coat a 9-inch bundt pan with cooking spray and dust with flour and pour mixture in. Bake for 40 to 45 minutes, until a toothpick inserted in the center comes out clean. Cake should be refrigerated. Let cool, and frost with cream cheese.

Banana Apple Muffins

Ingredients:
3 cups whole-wheat flour
2 cups water
2 ripe bananas
1 apple diced
1 teaspoon baking powder
1 teaspoon vanilla
1 egg
2 teaspoons peanut butter (unsalted natural)
¼ teaspoon cinnamon

Directions:

Preheat oven to 350 degrees. In a mixing bowl beat all ingredients until well blended, and pour into cupcake pans. You can use the cupcake paper liners or you can spray the pan with non-stick cooking spray. Bake for 20 minutes. If you would like to use these for a birthday party or special occasions, you can frost them with soft cream cheese.

Feline Ice Cream Treats

These are a nice little summer treats that your cat will love. I don't recommend that you go over-board with these; they should be used as a once in a while as a very special treat.

Banana Cantaloupe Freeze

Ingredients:
1 banana mashed
2 cups of smashed ripe cantaloupe
½ cup yogurt (plain, unsweetened)
1 teaspoon honey

Directions:

Blend banana, cantaloupe, honey and yogurt in a food processor. Pour into ice cube trays and freeze.

Blueberry Freeze

Ingredients:
1 cup yogurt (unsweetened, plain)
2 tablespoons honey
4 tablespoons blueberries
½ of banana

Directions:

Blend yogurt, honey, blueberries and banana in a food processor. Pour into ice cube trays and freeze.

Peanut Butter Freeze

Ingredients:
1 cup yogurt (unsweetened, plain)
1 teaspoon honey
3 tablespoons peanut butter (natural, unsalted)
½ cup applesauce

Directions:

Blend yogurt, honey, peanut butter, and applesauce in a food processor. Pour into ice cube trays and freeze.

These ice cream recipes can be used in an ice cream maker and served immediately.

BOOKS AVAILABLE BY THIS AUTHOR

Woofing it Down
The Quick & Easy Guide to Making Healthy Dog Food At Home

Lapping It up
The Quick & East Guide to Making Healthy Cat Food At Home

The Ultimate Yorkshire Terrier Book
Guide to Caring, Raising, Training, Breeding, Whelping, Feeding and
Loving a Yorkie

Tales of the Whosawhachits
Key Holders of the Realm (Book 1 of series)
Young Adult Novel
(YABI Award Winner)

Mirror Mirror
Seven Years Bad Luck
Adult Paranormal Fantasy Novel
(Covey Award Winner)

COMING SOON

Tales of the Whosawhachits
Enter the 5th Realm (Book 2 of series)
Young Adult Novel

Pecking it Up
Recipes for feeding your Parakeet, Cockatiel, Finch, Canary, Lovebird,
African Grey, Cockatoo, Conure, Dove, Lorie, Macaw, Quaker and
more

True Encounters with Imaginary Friends
Young Adult Novel